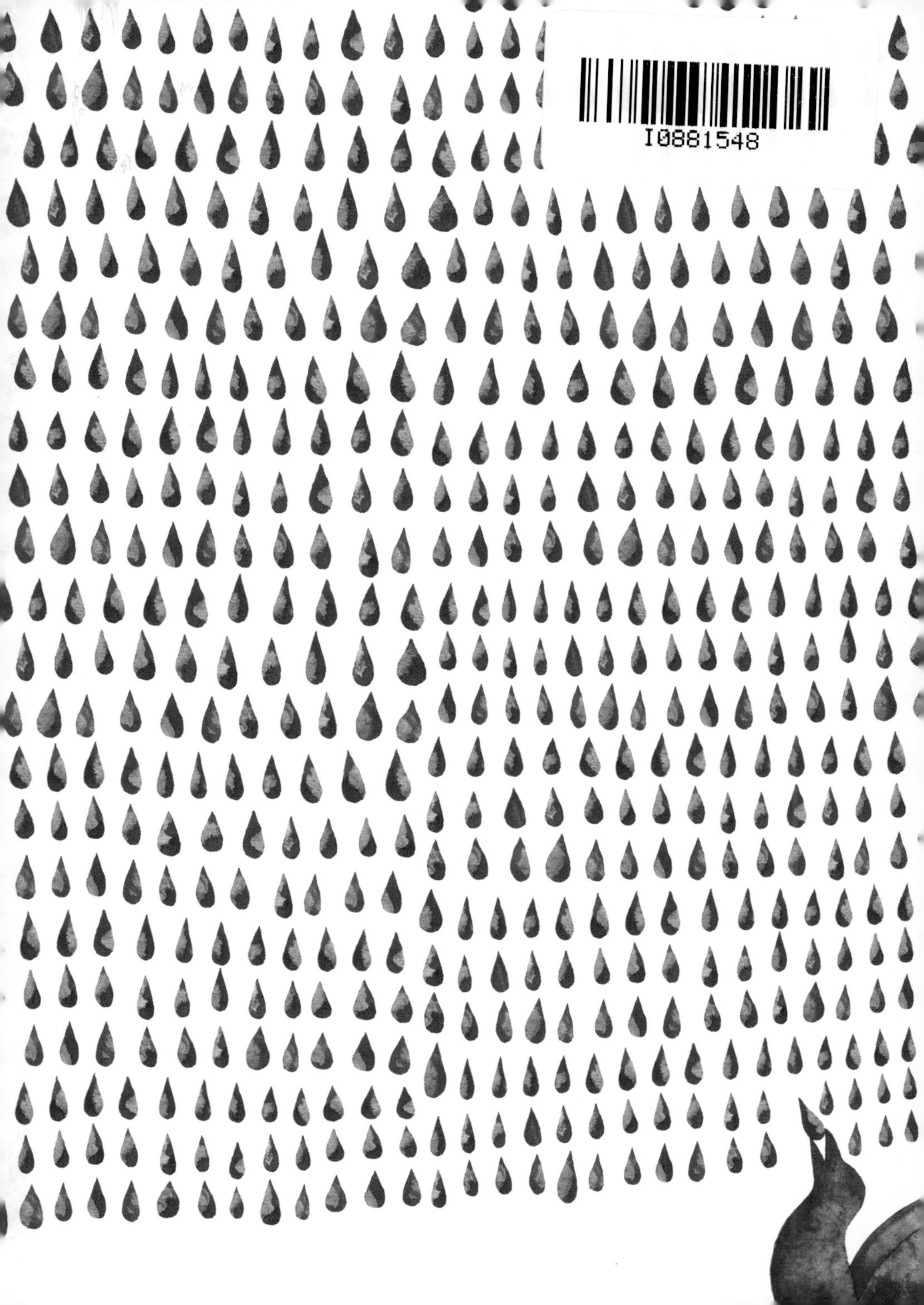

Natalka Marynchak

ANTIDESPAIRANT

Dedicated to the memory of people
who died as a result of the armed aggression
of the russian federation against Ukraine

Natalka Marynchak

ANTIDESPAIRANT

Graphics
Kostiantyn Zorkin

Kulturalis

#antidespairant

translated by Anna Antonova

here it is my deep green
the colour of grass and my old city
peeking out from last year's maple leaves
glimmering on rotting fences
like a jugular vein
breathing tranquillity
emanating
from enamelled lanterns
of the city's jumble sale
sprouting through the pavement cracks
the colour of the sun's eternal triumph
over winter and sadness
the colour that is lulling
healing
the colour of a dark and quiet river stream
otherworldly and routine
here is a ghostly antique mirror
green
here is mavka's[1] hair
she's hiding under a bent old tree
listening in
on the city's sounds with unfeigned interest
the colour is weaving together past and present
entwining
Kharkiv's streets
its dams
its scrolls
the cheekbones of its squares

[1]Mavka is a traditional Ukrainian folkloric image, a female spirit associated with nature and forest.

the arms of its trees
the furnaces of its flowers
weaving it all into one tapestry
of all that is real
grass is growing around the city
shaping its identity
praising its idea
asserting its glory

10.02.2022

but by the fifth day you can tell the distance by the sound
the sound of the enemy monster that wants blood
now murmuring and whistling and knocking are enemies to you
and we cut off conversations mid-word when we hear them

and we sleep and don't sleep but stay half-dreaming
each day we carry on our unfinished conversation
how are things with you
there's still milk I feed my child
I was outside the city I saw a cow torn in two
I see breadlines snaking out of my window
people are coordinated and focused
now I've got some bread and take medicine to mum
what are you doing where are you
in the city we sleep taking turns in the basement
and we keep an eye on the flag so that it isn't ripped down
I weep with pride for the fallen girls and boys
my clothes haven't dried out for a while
they've finally turned the power back on
ice cream for dinner no cartoons just yet
I understood today that war is an everyday word

how are you over there
we made some strong tea
something else
no
that's enough for us now
how is your wife doing
she's quiet and no longer wails
she bakes bread and whispers and mutters
I listened closely
she curses all the mothers
who raised their sons as lying rotten dogs
she keeps saying you should plant periwinkle on a grave
she keeps worrying that the candles lit in memory will go out

if the bastards knew who they've woken up
they haven't even dreamed of women
with assault rifles in formation
of unarmed fellow villagers stopping tank columns
of noble swaggering squads of the armed forces
of the thousands and millions ready to fight to the end
so that not a single crumb of our land is ceded
and a passionate desire to return home alive

what are you doing there
I've finished my cigarette
I'll talk to you later they're shooting
here a house and a daycare were blown apart
along with little children

no one could ever forgive something like that

how are things with you
we are sort of fine but still no power
a Grad[2] missile sticks out of the neighbour's house
like a scarecrow
today I bartered some dog food for bread
we're painting at home
we're only surviving through songs
when the bombing thunders we sing even louder
what's the most terrifying
the most terrifying is when the coveted silence
finally descends

28.02.2022

[2]BM-21 Grad ('Hailstorm') is a self-propelled rocket launcher developed in the Soviet Union and routinely used by russian armed forces in their attacks on Ukrainian territory.

snow falls mouldy on the black earth
it hides spring
war on earth another night
war is killing places that I love
snow is covering it
as a doctor in the operating room
administers an anaesthetic
snow is hiding the war from our eyes

Ukraine is hiding its children
but you can't hide anything from God
or from the snow
and it falls on the earth
and then you can't collect it
snow sows and sows
snow in march[3]
this winter's last argument
and then it will be
spring
and it'll be gone
the war

07.03.2022

[3]The author uses lower-case initial letters for all months to reflect the suspended sense of time in Ukraine since the full-scale invasion – as if time itself has stopped.

and every one of us will have her own war
dishevelled private
each person needed a wall
her own wall
to withstand
a wall of the university Derzhprom[4] city council
a wall that is the centre of the cosmos in your imagination
the centre of your own private rockslide
a place of power
a place of your downfall
a place of your awareness and patience
a place in which you lived and died
and finally defied death

everyone will have their own story
of beaten paths and bated breath
everyone will have their own settled territory
of roaring and laughter
now I have a heart
of reinforced concrete
it knows no pity
or comfort

09.03.2022

[4]Derzhprom, or the State Industry Building, is a cultural landmark in Kharkiv – an office building built in the Constructivist style in 1928. In October 2024, it sustained significant damage from russian bombing.

O God here
our spines
are becoming water jets
we flow as waterfalls
become rivers
become icy lakes
the earth is drenched in us
our mountains also
escalate with ridges
our spines are everywhere now
in every tree and high place
these axles stand tall

O God let us
remain on earth
where lie all of our ancestors
let us survive
gritting our teeth
feel like the roots from the earth
support the leaves
in every rustle
in every movement
remain on earth
where my graves are near

remain on earth
where my great-grandmother's house is near
sense the earth sighing
wearily at night
sleep girl
something flew past

16.03.2022

I'm spending this war
on the Lord's knee
when the thundering is too loud He whispers
breathe
you are a free beloved child
look here sit close by
all My children
who dared just to breathe
and who have not lost their faith
this depth allows one to love one's earth
this depth gives direction to one's actions
teaches one not to shut one's eyes and to live

I'm spending this war sitting on the Lord's knee
and now I know that He was always holding my hand
while I fought back and held still without a sound
He held and held my hand
while awaiting our parting

translated by Kevin Reese

17.03.2022

translated by Natalya Sukhonos

the children of war had children
so that those children would have children
those first children didn't want those third children
to have black dreams
the first ones wanted quiet
the second children never thought they'd
be more resilient than concrete
they built cities
lived their life
processed their generational traumas
so that those third ones would not twitch in their dreams
the third ones were born under the calm
and under the sky that burns and whips
the first and the second and the third
cry and laugh
imbibe their identity
understand the deep faith of their people
realise their greatness
the first and the second children are like ants
each pushes their grain of sand
so that the third ones would no longer fear
looking at the sky
through their hands
through a loophole
the Sky bends to the earth
and kisses every one of its children

18.03.2022

all our dead stand behind us
pray in all the world's languages
God we were forged by time
we're a gigantic net from the living hedge
each one connected to each one
and no one thinks of washing one's hands of it
we're one whole
the dead the alive and the future ones
everyone knows their own
most important note of the army lute
everyone plays it
as if he had come comes and will come only for this
God now you already know what will come of this
all our dead and all our unborn
are closing the sky with their love
so that those who stand on earth
will have enough love and anger
to withstand achieve and defeat
the rotten bones of the enemy
God
we are all in your palms
so understandable
and not easy

19.03.2022

translated by Natalya Sukhonos

translated by Anna Antonova

enemy my enemy
close your weary eyes
enemy my enemy
you won't survive the night

enemy my enemy
let your mother wait
enemy my enemy
she'll know the truth too late

enemy my enemy
your last breath you drew
enemy my enemy
hear death call for you

hear it calling for you
hear it calling wailing
enemy my enemy
your sleep-death is waiting

waiting and waiting
no more need to wait
enemy my enemy
your death is at the gate

29.03.2022

my river has coffee and a leisurely waterfront
devastated shores
my river has seen many wars
but it says once this one is over
come and I'll hold you
by this water
thick stems are growing
of goosefoot and reed
roads and hidden pathways lead
along this river

children and grown-ups soldiers and weirdos
gather here to see
a bird land on the water
sunlight glimmer in the deep
mavkas grin
cold and fiery
stinging wounds heal
draining of pus

this river
in this heart of our city
will always have place
for words and music
for joy and grief
this water will take it all in
wash it anew
and here are you
sitting down on this shore
wounded and heavy
you get up again
and you have no bounds any more
you encompass it all
this river with both of its shores
and this city as well

01.04.2022

translated by Anna Antonova

finally night frosts are retreating
everything gives in and bends towards this spring
flowers are coming towards the light
from the earth

the earth is thrown open
black and friendly
and the flower goes through the earth
like your prayer
from heart to heart

the heart indeed beats
beats although it sees clenches and cries out
beats and turns to stone and carries the truth
beats and gathers itself to strength truth and faith
beats because who if not you
must grow a flower
cultivate hope
cry out these tears
shelter everyone who you love

the heart holds its difficult defence
the human body doesn't know its border
the heart-stone of the great constant tower
more than a year or two will pass
until someone lets it go
until someone covers with dust the inconsolable wasteland
until you gather all the tears into a woollen handkerchief
and embark with these treasures
to those worlds
where your friends are strong and young
where all your loved ones are alive
and embraces are warm
where an adolescent spindly boy runs out

the neighbour's son
intact
without any marks on his body of holes or tyres
and you will embrace
as if this is communion
as if God has poured out your portion of happiness
and you will go into the whole unbroken peaceful home

the heart will finally breathe out
it will rest
the buzz of spring will rise over everything

05.04.2022

translated by Anna Antonova

our embroideries
are like red scars on white skin
wounds cut into with shards of glass
splinters of steel
lumps of concrete
see the bird right here
it's red
it's the incoming
that got to me
that my great-grandmother remembers
here's a black line
a long furrow
the black burn of the black sowing season
my ancestor's black sorrow
for my own woe

and here she says are my roots
over these red lesions
over these black burns
the body tortured and torn
we'll plant the most beautiful
most painful flowers
and I don't resist for long
I take the yarn and needle
and I start embroidering

here's my land
here's my long road
here's a hill of sprouting flowers
here's the water we couldn't waste
here's the melted snow we drank
here's the fire that gave us life
here's my blood
flowing back to the old world

here's my body
bending

oh Lord
I will keep embroidering
all my people's pain
living it
we are all strung together by this thread
here's the trace of my perseverance, red
here's the trace of my power, black
and all my victorious flowers
that will cover our land and these hearts of ours
with tender petals
thin spouts lithe stems
translucent veils
sturdy ribs

06.04.2022

translated by Anna Antonova

here she is
brewing tea and getting last year's preserves
from the cellar
glossy blackcurrant mashed with sugar
fingers struggling
to open the jar

she takes out a gilt-edged dish
fine china
the kind you won't find today
it sings along with each movement
her hands are shaking
so it won't stop singing

she wraps a kerchief around her head
ivory with blue flowers
her daughter's gift from last year
why didn't she wear it before
it looks so pretty

here is someone at the door
knocking so loudly
her temples start hurting
she doesn't want to but still goes to answer
it's dark outside
like the sunrise won't come any more
here she is
lying collapsed by the door
her flowers no longer blue
they are blooming in red

08.04.2022

> And the Lord said, 'Simon, Simon! Indeed, Satan has asked for you, that he may sift you as wheat. But I have prayed for you, that your faith should not fail; and when you have returned to Me, strengthen your brethren.' Luke 22: 31–32

translated by Kevin Reese

Saint Peter is joining the chat
oh Peter where have you been for so long
we longed for you
you recall how you thrice denied God
and He sprouted just the same
from heart to heart
oh Peter your help is critical
for one who for forty days has not laughed
for one who doesn't know whether to live or to gutter out
you can remind him
just why God gave you the keys
oh Peter where are you out there
don't be silent

and Saint Peter types in the answer
to all those who are in vaults or the metro
to all those who believe in the armed forces
and territorial defence

once I was called Simon
and the Word protected me from utmost despair
'I have prayed for you, that your faith should not fail'
I thought if Jesus prayed for me
then why am I giving myself up
and my heart and head were filled with light
and then it became clear
that I am no longer Simon
but Peter the Rock
on me stand the faith and the temple and the church

all is built on me
just like each one of you
there in the darkness
is a little stone of truth
is a hearth of faith
and Jesus himself prays for each of you
just as he once prayed for me
and I pray for each one who has come to me
this is what our faith is building on
on great love
for which there exists no measure
well that's all now I must run
I have an evening shift
I have to give out body armour to our guys
so that they stay alive
so that I can meet them in heaven after fifty years or so

10.04.2022

who is this
it's my son
standing here by my grave
he is six
I was tortured and killed

who is this
it's my mother
she was gathering snow
that could have helped us survive
she was in a hurry
and

who is this
it's my daughter
who barely made it
to the edge of the ravine
she'll keep singing forever now

who is this
it's my other son
who is twenty
he's learned how to shoot
and is dreaming of bullets
that are hitting their targets
for everyone
tortured and killed

who is this
it's a man
who is hugging his cat
he's alone
no one else made it out
just him and the darkness inside

the cat's glare
lights up his night
dark and covered in slush

who is this
the ones who are going to survive
through this war
their hearts filled with gratitude and pain
pride and loneliness
victorious joy
compassion and steadfast resolve
and I want you to be
one of them

15.04.2022

the second month of the eighth year of war
embrace me embrace me embrace
the battle lasts three centuries
three centuries and eight years
and a few dozen days
the remains of quiet dreams have lifted off somewhere
in the fresh air
and one unfinished today is left for all

I don't know numbers
and no one knows numbers
it's only clear that it's day fifty-two
it's only clear that night has flickered
and therefore has passed
are you alive asks the abandoned cat
alive

I respond
no one needs abandoned house cats
no one needs women who seem stronger
wind will move dust
like quiet
embrace me the one who
can withstand my pain
the pain I had before the hour of war
the pain for all the anticipated losses
the pain for all those abandoned cats
the pain for all those who had gone
and for those who will come back

embrace me the one
who will know that only
quietly you could break through smoothly made armour

translated by Natalya Sukhonos

return me return me return me to your mirror
and don't you dare say your 'I love you'

the second month of the eighth year of war
I am the earth under the feet
protect me
embrace me

16.04.2022

on the worn-out floor of my church
I can see birds and hearts
fish and clouds
light descends on this worn-out floor
hundreds and thousands have been here before
they are coming today
they'll keep coming

all I can do now
is stand on this floor
and think
that He will protect our loved ones
that He will protect them
the One who knows
what it means
to stand up and believe

our generals stand on this floor
our soldiers
and volunteers
police officers
doctors and writers
musicians and poets
our regular people
the code of our nation
the people who long for
quiet and freedom
and these people will have it
because they are too stubborn
I'm here for an hour
but my church, it knows
each one of its children
its floor is worn out

17.04.2022

translated by Anna Antonova

you'll remember who visited you in war
who came and said
come here I'll hold you
who stayed silent and raging
who hid their tears behind your shoulders
why are you crying
there's only one reason
that all of us share

I am hiding our food in three places
I am watching the flag over the city
I am brewing coffee same place every day
I am recording air raid strikes
driving all over the place
I am Saltivka's[5] big black eyes
I am Oleksiivka's[6] jagged scars
I am the intersection of Myronosytska and Svobody[7]
bends and twists
of this city's parks and hills
I am the one who picks up a shard
out of a coffin
I am waiting
until I can meet my unburdened dreams
I am waiting for my suburb to be freed
I know you're somewhere here
I am the green leaves of this spring
you'll remember every meeting
every priceless movement
we are all guardians of this city

[5]Saltivka is a large residential area in Kharkiv that suffered significant damage from the russian army's shelling in spring 2022.

[6]Oleksiivka is a residential neighbourhood in Kharkiv.

[7]Myronosytska and Svobody are the names of streets in central Kharkiv; both have suffered extensive damage during the war.

until the enemy is defeated
we all hear Kharkiv's voice
we all stand on guard
like an ouroboros[8]

17.04.2022

[8] An ancient symbol of a snake eating its own tail; it represents the natural cycle of life, death and renewal.

do you know what I want the most God
that fires would occur because of negligence
like before
that flowers would bloom and warm rays of light
that we wouldn't have to raise money for
someone's thermal imager
and instead we would just come together
to hold our loved ones in white-hot embrace

you know God every time in every conversation
I learn how much I need
I want to speak and not stumble on every word
I want to contemplate silver mists again
I want to unlearn how to tally and hide food
I want to ride at night
order a double latte in the old town
I want to just laugh when something is funny
forget the keys on that side of the door
I want to just talk and just be silent
so that the inner censor would not stand watch

do you know how much we need to pronounce and say
and we don't have time for any of it
you know give it to us, this time
I will spend it very carefully
without fuss and unnecessary commotion
you know God give us all quiet
the quiet that we had earlier
with the creak of trolley cars around six a.m.

and the bells of the trams
now we don't have enough
of these simple and regular things
come quicker
I've already brewed some tea

21.04.2022

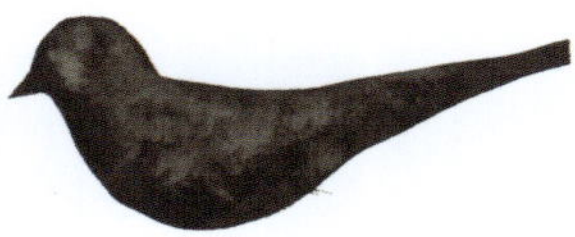

here they are shooting at our hearts
while we keep walking crawling and walking
no end in sight
we cut out bullets from our hearts
our hearts don't need to restart
and we ask our doctors while in recovery
when can I return to the ranks
why am I stuck out here
while our boys are preparing to fight

here are our sisters mothers and brides
each one with her own kind of witchery
each one quietly whispering
warding off evil
each one knows a secret spell
that brings you back by daybreak alive and well
that sees you safe through the battlefield
turns each blade of grass into a shield
leads you back to the medics with lead in your heart
keeps it from failing

so we know no fear and no regret
all our ancestors speak inside our heads
as we strike our skill from ash and stone
our spirit is born within our bones
and each one of our own
has a mighty heart
that no matter how much you shoot
will keep beating

22.04.2022

my houses and my Sloboda[9] huts
in this war
bare their spines
reveal their deep-hidden ribs
shake in the wind like bare stems

each one of these houses and huts is mine
in each one a star descends
I cast a spell
on each stone and clump of dust
like a sick child

look above you stars have risen at night
the wind sweeps out grief
from all streets and squares
the moon is flooding everything in its light
this airstrip will heal
and will be good again for landing

listen to each rustle of corn growing
listen how grass chooses direction at crossroads
listen to birds
listen to the universe singing
only you can hear it others won't know it

each spine and rib and each little stone
will puncture the enemy's throat
like a bone
bitter tarragon
dry earth
our earth won't want you to mix with it
won't accept your rot

translated by Anna Antonova

[9]Sloboda Ukraine, or Slobozhanshchyna, is a historic region in northeastern Ukraine that traditionally includes Kharkiv, Sumy and Luhansk Oblasts.

will wipe out your very seed
disperse scatter dissolve
into a scary tale of old
nightly terrors dark windows sinister ghosts
death will appear to you
under the clouds and on the ground
it will come to graze and eat
you won't know whether to lie or sit
whether you lie or fly or sit or run
death knows no bounds

every tear of my land
of my child
will be a nail in the enemy's coffin
a hammer blow on the enemy's head
a terrible wound
a wheezing sound in the enemy's throat

get off my land run away leave it behind
know nothing in your life but misfortune
know no one in your life but betrayal
no easy death and what it was for
it will be
it will come
it'll take out your life through your eye
the eye that could see no beauty
kill them all don't show them pity
kill them all for my tears houses huts
take it slow
they don't deserve to go easy

22.04.2022

the thin edge of the dark sky
the loops of my kerchief's weaving
everything I see from the window
the murmuring shoots of the apricots
april showers
april spring dews

flashes that blind the eyes for a long time
and crazy enormous stars
I'm lying down and imagining how the sky is stitched anew
with waves of rain
tender mists
thin light clouds
I sense the warmth of your hand
as if it appears not just in my imagination
I am here on this earth in the same home
I sleep on the pallet it smells like wood
you still want to be with me
I no longer have any restrictions
or the instinct of self-preservation

do you remember when you used to be able to
stop on Svobody Square[10]
underneath the lanterns
in the dark car
I would like to become the us
that we were then
I would yell to her
don't run
stay
don't rush
speak

translated by Natalya Sukhonos

[10]A square in central Kharkiv that was severely hit by russian missiles in March 2022. The name means 'Freedom Square'.

and of course she would say
I'm leaving now
and we would never see each other again
not to contemplate now flashes that blind
not hear the thunder that takes away your energy
not sense the earth tremble
in solitude

24.04.2022

but if everything is truly different and I should forget
should let go of all those who forgot about me
should let go of all those who gifted me sadness
should sit myself down on a hilltop and
contemplate the green hum

but if there is truly only you and your loneliness
there is no one else connected to it or to you
if someone will summon or call you from there
it'll be clear at once that it's not him or her
his or her eyes don't fit me at all
his or her hands don't suit me
here mirror reflections bear witness for me
my imagined prison misses my presence

here I'm alone amidst the throng and the crowd
I wish someone would come
or would it be a disaster then
step away from me stranger you're too close to me
and everyone's leaving or left
whose pain you were carrying in your hand
whose pain you were rocking to sleep
for someone it was too much for someone not enough
here I was I stood now I'm gone

there on the hilltop it's so far away oh as far as you can get
quiet it's so quiet
and the grass is green green
the redstart sings and dissolves all sad thoughts
you should come sometime and at least look at me

24.04.2022

translated by Kevin Reese

the ocean is murmuring inside of us
you and me
that same one
age-old
that we could always smell somewhere
beyond Derzhprom
waves crashing over North Saltivka
we put careless looming seashells
of empty black windows and beams
to our ears and listen
what do they tell you those seashells
so many feelings within

the ocean is beside us
as it always has been
ruffling my hair
ignoring my sadness
unlike us, it knows only one itinerary
just be here
touch our faces
where features of our ancestors
are shining through
chiselled carved plain tough
reminding us
that everything comes from love
and no one dares ignore its call

here are my eyes
like the eyes of all women who came before
who saw our bread and freedom taken away
and loved this land
of periwinkles and other blooms
who could cast a spell to heal a wound
or embroider a long happy road ahead

for the family they loved
they are sending me signs
with my blossoming gardens
those who never forgot how the last breadcrumb tastes
those who taught me to plant and water and bake
silently since they were never with me
in reality
what they passed on to me is the pride in my blood
and an unbroken stubborn heart
they whispered to me at night
my girl there is so much love
learn to see it and not to waste
here it rests
hiding in these green leaves
under this white snow
sprouting in green stalks
baking in a loaf of bread
running to you swishing its tail
like a cat
we left so much of it for you
you'll see

28.04.2022

in my garden the flowerheads sway
cats squint their eyes and dash wildly
we know they say that you bring good fortune
here you've got some cat food so why are you crying
I'm not crying
I'm just swallowing air
and it's not passing through
it's burning
it's getting stuck in my heart
how many chords are there in the world
but I myself only have thirds
what are you doing
I am continuing to plant my gardens
every bush and tree into the earth
so that there will be less misfortune
more air
more

each root is wrapped into spells
each stem so that light would lay down
only from heavenly bodies
only to free oneself from doubts and hesitations
that there is beauty in everything
even when it seems that beauty
is gone

let these flowers trees and bushes that will be left in this earth
each time remind us of each spring
what it was like to plant them without sleeping
what it was like to whisper and speak to them
you have to withstand to stand
you have to flower and give birth
so that after many years little children

under garlands of light and flowers
can shout and be joyful
can just be and just live

you open your eyes and continue to walk quietly
where are you going today the cats ask silently
but I don't yet know where
it's easier to go out into the great world like this
to pluck at the strands of its strange nets
someone will get you everything you ask for
why are you standing there not taking it

no matter where you set out to
make it to the goal
cats make a sign of the cross behind my back
meow with squinted eyes quietly
and sit at the threshold
whispering to each other
in that quiet the tags on their collars
clink so eloquently

29.04.2022

everything that holds us is our land and prayer
invisible wings green shoots
my heart is Pandora's box
if you open it beware
pain will crawl out
look around everywhere
see our steppes and woods
wail with a merciless glare
it's not looking for mountains
it only wants plains
everything that holds us is only this day
what happens then
a feast or a grave
will I wake up as birdsong or silence
what will I leave behind me
everything that holds us is the last miraculous word
give me the strength
not to deny You and love
oh Lord
to stand up and keep standing
to sleep without dreams
to fight my wrath
everything that holds us
is so primal so brittle
you know I am not made of steel

here is my land and my suffering city
full of ruins but clean
ashes next to neon signs
joy and death
here is my land and my heart within
it laughs and cries
everything that holds us is sets of opposites
but the city stays
rain or shine
and I am staying imaginary or alive

01.05.2022

translated by Anna Antonova

the night comes on like it's the only place where you can be
curled up like a snail in the middle of the room
someone else's heart has tried to force me to sleep
and what came of that
it would be better not to know

I listen to the booming and I listen to the spaces in between
what's wrong with you
it's these echoes of silence and pain
it's that I can hear the enemy reloading

I listen onward
but onward everything goes quiet
what's wrong with you
it's like I'm dying a little
how did this happen
I don't know I don't know I don't know
this is my city and I'm leaving it
there's my dacha and way over there are my hills
and we used to make trips out that way to fish

and here's my second city
again I'm packing my bags
who am I now
where am I going and why
cars are passing by outside
streets and garages
high-rise buildings and parks
what I have to do is get everyone I love
out of here
and then
this time I'll go back

translated by John Wright

my heart always knew everything
you can hear it even in childhood
it wept it pounded hard and then it was silent
as many times as I've had to start over
that's how many times they've refused to stamp my papers
my heart heard it all
I thought it was giving up
but it goes on beating
despite what can't be made peace with

night covers everyone
the sun goes out
the light goes out
the candles burn down slowly
the heart goes on beating out its most intriguing rhythms
with skips
and flutters
it beats for the cities unconquered that stand
it beats for the shrouds of the martyrs
missing in unploughed fields

03.05.2022

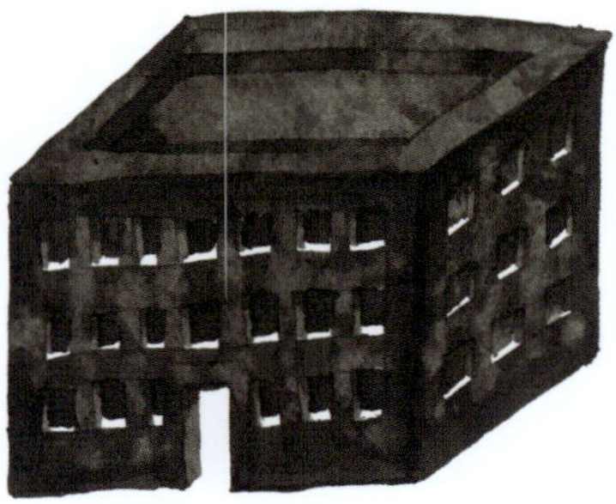

my heart is like a flower
just as tender with weightless transparent petals
it trembles the same way
the same way it bends down to the earth
the same way it cries each evening and morning
and steadfastly gets through the day

my heart is like the earth
just as rich and black
just as deep and dark
the very same winds roll my specks of dust here and there
just as fecund for love and flowers
an abyss cut by deep crevasses languishes with it
and if it cannot love it will disappear
it'll turn to ash

my heart is like the sky
just as borderless and boundless
just as tender
just as fickle
now fading now rejoicing
now pouring rain

my heart has nowhere to hide from war and pain
and why has it chosen to be yours and with you
here it trembles and closes its eyes tight
here it falls and takes flight
to tell the truth it's been long since I understood
just why it holds
me up

04.05.2022

translated by Kevin Reese

at night only animals walk around freely
loosen their wild tails
knock their paws on the gates
why have you not yet become a wild fox
why are you choosing the middle of the fence
and lying down until dark
why are you forgetting who you are

at night the animals walk into the house quietly quietly
woman come on get up open all the doors and windows
spring is outside the fence
do everything you're used to
plant flowers
carry water
teach us how to value freedom once more
teach every flower and every feather of every bird
direct every flutter of our hair

at night the wind is harsh
at night the animals are tender and wild
their eyes sparkle they are reconciled
with the thick wind
the silver light of the moon is slowly descending
it sits beside me
hello
tell us more fairy tales about this bumbling world
and the miracle begins
here hair that is broken by war
grows again
with a swing of an eyelash

it becomes fur
here all the fences are opening
and the fog of the narratives fills the quiet earth

the animals sit in a circle
without making a campfire
instead of fire a bitter love brewed on wormwood lights their way
tell us
what do they say about
the river meeting another and lingering to the sea
tell a tree about the changes to its bark
the smallest seedling about how it clings to the earth with its
roots
tell the animals about how darkness rolls to the palate
and flows in the breast as deliberate patience

and they wait
until the woman gets up and goes to make miracles
you had never been alone you hear me
you had never been alone
you had never been

04.05.2022

translated by Kevin Reese

dandelions gutter out towards the evening
bow their heads politely in the darkness
throwing up their hands
greet the setting sun
and fall asleep

the noise of the jetty heals wounds
healing water washes against my shores
the river speaks
and tenderly touches my fingers
listen

take all my sorrows oh dark water
all my realisations and take up my sufferings
carry away my pain
wash them from me please
wash them away

and the river narrows its eyes
sends me black birds on the water
delicate frogs that take up their nuptial songs
reeds nod their heads
everything goes in tenuous waves
water
grass
wind
sound
the river stills my breathing and my heartbeat
slows
frees me here
I am
and the war is
and the river is
we all exist together
and each of us is already tired
of existing

06.05.2022

the current of this love is so deep-sea
that no one who has blundered into it knows about it
you can only guess behind the haze of embraces
behind the veil of their gradual disappearance
behind the way that the shadow of darkness
disappears behind the eyes
common swifts are giving away

all the bitterness of this love
soaring so high
and whistling and speaking so incisively
beware of this love
yet be this love
here's the blue dawn
here's the hazy evening
here's her wrapping around the shoulders like water
and her memory and depth are not accessible
to any of the sentences
any of the phrases
any of the letters
it pulses so deep
as deep as the jugular vein can reach
as the most hidden precipice in the world can reach
its current is the most underwater of all currents
it is worth all the predictions and objections
it is worth all the inappropriate pauses

who knows about it who knows about its origins
only a ray of light
that shines on the newly woven spiderweb
only those that had never not for the world
remained alone

07.05.2022

translated by Natalya Sukhonos

translated by John Wright

there's an alternate universe for those with strength of heart
when you're under heavy fire and an angel blows
on the back of your neck
and protects you
and no longer conceals his wings
and on that foggy morning at last you can see his outline
as you look for notes from your family while you have barely any signal

there's an alternate universe for those that look death
right in the eye
without blinking
and death turns away
seeing the strength of a woman
death turns tails when it learns
how much strength there is here
how much love
it walks away grinding its teeth saying
'I will be back for you'
and she snaps at it as it walks away
'A few decades from now
I'll call for you myself
I'll bake you some bread
but not today
and not during this
greatest of wars'

an alternate universe
brewing the tastiest coffee in the cutest of mugs
finding the strength for a smile as I tenderly think of the fallen
watching the redstarts go hopping about as they flick their tailfeathers
writing my memories in detail
thinking of new names for the streets in Kharkiv

streets that are bitter and silver

08.05.2022

here are my days
they come like petals from flower heads
here are my nights rolling like dark waves
they stretch like tar
petals are dripping red on the floor

everyone is allotted exactly as many petals
as they can carry
everyone is given the same petals that make up the world
the worlds are different
the petals are different
one thing is the same
you have to carry them until the end
but they scatter
flutter in the wind
take off with a quiet cold wind
fly off with the slightest movement

you remember that very petal
weightless and tender
blood-red
as soon as it took off and flew
you had no knack for the others
but your strength hadn't gone anywhere
carry your petals
adorn our lives with them
until you can reach the end
and then he will stay there
he who will speak
I am waiting for so long
and you will understand
that there are no more petals

10.05.2022

translated by Natalya Sukhonos

what do the saints bring us in their trunk-like books
what is hiding there in the treasures enfolded by the heart
it's as if every saint is saying throw out everything unnecessary
look me in the face
everything that was and everything that will happen
will happen to establish greatness
will happen to establish your faith
will happen to win against stubbornness and time
will not happen at the same time

what do their faces carry simple canonical features
from the beginning of the war it seems like each one is crying
but just like us in the thick of events
without tears
in the same way the juice of the tree gathers
for a long time into a fresh cut
and we fill invisible rivers with our tears
and when the dam bursts
no medicine will come in handy
we don't cry strutting dark news
we're silent listing our sadnesses
and are broken by simple sentences
I miss you so much
as if you had never felt a greater expression of pain
what do the saints respond to this
I'm with you

11.05.2022

but with the cold wind there comes strong grass
sharp bitter and green
the kind that can bear this cold and this darkness
the kind that's stronger than oak ash and maple
the kind that can cover the foxholes
or bind up the most painful wounds
the kind so good for falling into with someone you love
here it is that grass moving with the wind
like a deep green sea
when the war moves away from the edge of our city
you and I will be able to fall onto that green grass
not counting the bruises and breaks
                                        all the cuts and the slaughter
we'll be falling and putting an end to the heat of exhaustion
I'll ask if you have a home
no home
but falling into the green of the grass I'll inform you
I'm at home
I shall answer

grow oh you green grass
despite all the doings of men
despite death and despair
we just can't get enough of your green little statements
that life is worth more

11.05.2022

what will save you
quiet living water
that flows through all obstacles in your city
during this Easter church processions were not possible
so water had done this for us
and now our thoughts are clean enough
we are now green and plucked like spring leaves
like leaves that broke through all frosts in february
and through cold
as if to cover with themselves the dark bases of their home
branches
as if to cover with themselves everyone who will not have
strength there
to place the amulets of your nests by the lines

what will save you
a cross clutched in your fist
what will not allow you to cry yourself out
sitting on a chair
the only one that survived
we started a garden
we live in a neighbour's car
to leave
but how will we leave from here
you see grandpa is slowly digging out the cellar
it will be enough for the two of us

what will save you
my miraculous war gardens
every day I conscientiously plant them and stay silent
my children will not know
but my grandchildren will understand everything
these are grandmother's tears that are flowering and abound
so fruitfully

how many tears do I hide every day and how much sorrow
in order to smile in the middle of city crowds
in order to watch my hills and hillocks
to pretend that we can't at all hear the trumpet of lilacs
what will save me
the warm lighthouse of the candle pilot light
I will submit to it
a ship of reed
and it will flutter
let it be so
because without it we can't see anything

13.05.2022

translated by Kevin Reese

clean up clean up the broken glass
it's like everything you and I had is broken
it's like the last friends and the last drops
of my patience
sweep up sweep up the smashed deformed shop windows
the squashed oranges lemons
the squashed yearnings and hopes
only you can
put the still-living flame into the tomb
well go ahead and dam me up
with all the shells of all your bombings
it's really like it's the one thing that brings you happiness
just don't ask later
where I have all this pain from
and why it's increasing
and why I'm not waiting for anything
except for betrayal
there is no longer any trust in me
are you happy

sweep up
sweep up the glass and the memory
do every stupid thing that they tell you to
pick at all the fresh scars
to better recall these days
to not hear what the dead are saying
these could be the final minutes
hold on to her
hand in hand

15.05.2022

instead of our Bibles and Psalters we pick up our phones
that show all the road signs and every street that's closed
and as we pray we squeeze in our fists that hunk
of plastic and iron
stifling our deep groans and memories amid these kindling-days

instead of bread and wine we yearn for so much
as a cracker and clean water
save me and my freedom
from every nook
from every stage
from every phone
save me my God
'cause I shall stand here till I die
defending this city
maintaining the barrier
who are you He asks
but I don't know how to answer
I'm the one that cannot sleep or eat
I'm the one that finds the light
where standing is frightening and so is sitting
I'm the one that gets himself together and goes
the one with too much love
for this factory this country and this city

16.05.2022

translated by John Wright

finishing everything that's been taking forever
drags on like an old movie from before the war
casting you out of today to some bottom
and you try
you crush all your tasks into a couple of free hours
and only one of them won't move
wait
and you wait
you hang out the uneven white cloth of the day
but the task doesn't move
and continues to draw the juices from you
like it's pressing grapes into a young wine
what's that there behind the helplessness
behind the unfinished and unjustified hopes and days
I should be used to this feeling by now
and come to my senses

what's with us
look at these white days and black nights
look at these flashes that blind our eyes
look at this who knows how many tons of broken glass
this wall that's still standing
this door half off its hinges
this yard that you still can't go into
this debris
the homeless
that you're glad to see because they're alive
these cats
the dishes in the sink since february
this book with a page folded down
everything that strangles you
how are you
how are you
how are you

18.05.2022

translated by John Wright

she was here
the quiet water of her eyes swam on the great water
she stood and spoke
spring
here's a river that will for sure overflow
no matter who would restrict it
no matter who would ask
she gets up and leaves
because God had commanded it

she will get up from her sleep
she will throw off the cover of winter fogs
she will take off the fierce shackles of february
and go to the city
and will talk to the city dwellers
and finally they will hear

I am a river that flows and flows
and knows no borders
at some point there had been a river crossing
here and also a market
at some point on one side there had been workshops
on another side there had been merchants
and they were all busy doing something
and loved water and these convolutions
I am a river that will cover you with its coolness
and tugging warmth
I am that which you always have and have always had
I am the heart of your city
I am the flickering rapid canvas of your hearts
although you say
that ferroconcrete replaces the heart
I know better
what makes up your hearts

where all of this love comes from
and where all of this longing comes from
beyond my currents and tributaries

and that only to the city do you come so slowly
fall on me with streams and currents
you and I are what is really unbroken in this city
although who but I can really tell you about this
here you come and I offer my womb
and the mansion of shores
and every Kharkiv dweller has the memory
of my waters
this is exactly why you come back
this is exactly why you come here
under my bridges and gentle shores
this is exactly why you chant
my spring don't go

20.05.2022

what had made you alive
the time that oozed out from under the wheels
and made up the scroll of thoughts
the quiet that had throbbed with waves
when we had inhabited it
at some point we had lived in quiet and calm
should I put a question mark here or an exclamation mark
from what could we have warmed our palms
and fluttered our wings
throughout this war I had swept off so much grime from myself
so many unspoken thoughts and wishes
and aspirations
once you were also so thirsty for another's death

what to do with us afterwards
with those of us who had tolerated a ton of others' tears
who healed with embraces
who gave away everything we had
what to do with those who traded love for a curse
at the uncomfortable unprofitable rate
here is my millionth love
give me one word
only one word
so that he who came to my earth was glued to the spot like tin

what made you alive
the trembling of the earth
when it's not clear whether you'll finally become shadow
or you will remain here among darkness and candles
or you will turn to weapons
or you will find a hook
skilfully screwed into the last surviving beam
who were you before
a warrior or a fisherman

I was a fisherman's net
that had been forgotten on a birch tree
I hung myself in march
when foreign and dirty people came to my village
I couldn't bear it
I didn't know how it would be

what will they do with us being the way we are
where is it written how we should be forgiven
how we should be sung over and buried
how we then should be loved the way we are

what had made you alive
the stubbornness of a house cat
every night it told fortunes of a new day
and purred
come on don't remember yesterday
come on

23.05.2022

in this war we've donned our best
coral beads and ducats
who were our interlocutors and observers
just grey walls
just scavengers of broken pieces and remains
we went and thought
whether this were the last spring
or the last day
but the war filled us up once again
and gave us new songs and old

we've worn crosses and talismans on our bodies
we've embroidered ancient all-powerful codes
so that no one could see
could steal our hearts
that were beating and beat now in their striving for freedom
we were so beautiful in our going
only in dark times so many beautiful things are born
from sunken eyes and graven lines
from expressive wrinkles
from dusty faces eaten at by the wind
it's impossible to turn away
this earth has a way to care for the best of us
how to summon it

love

oh mama are we truly this beautiful only in war
after forty years a little child will ask someone
what is the most noble in those faces
and that someone will answer
come here for a hug
you see the flag in the window
it flies blue and yellow
it gave us beauty and strength that spring

23.05.2022

translated by Kevin Reese

here you're waking up in one of the most beautiful cities
without alarm clocks
without the first ray of sun
without tenderness
you're waking up to get up and go out
to keep moving forward

how you calculated earlier
today is Sunday
tomorrow the fasting will be completed
how you are calculating now
it's day ninety-something
if only no one would die
if only there were no news of a child who perished
if only there would be no last names you know
from A to Z
if only the blast wave heralded springtime
and were not the one that kills at a distance

you're waking up
the sun hasn't yet been able to set
but everyone is striving to get to it
and you
you also depend on the sun
though it seems it got stuck in february
how to calculate those non-existent months
by experience
unknown and acquired
what have you learned to do
to hold on to what earlier you didn't have in your hand
to not guess what will be there
in the end

you're waking up to sort out your stones
and the day shows you backroads of hopes
and you'll be able to fall asleep
squeezing all the love of the world
in your fist

01.06.2022

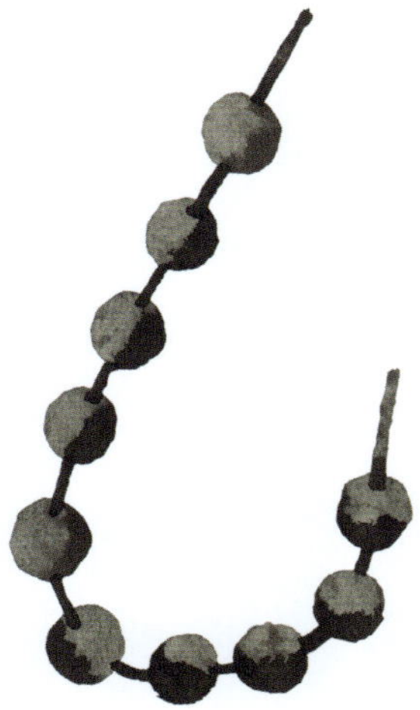

every night I repeat names
all the names I know
keep them safe God give them full strength

keep Maksym Serhii Andrii Artem
Oleh Serhii Serhii Savva
Oleksandr Mariana Anna Maria
the newborn Dmytro
the sick Olena
the sick Oleksii safe
keep them all safe
every one whom Your hand can touch
every one for whom You are the last hope
and keep Nadiia who is expecting also safe
keep them all safe you hear me

a whole country of ripe names that have to endure
endure and survive
give them firmament under their feet
give them the strongest embraces
and to those who won't surrender let them
let them be close by with those reliable ones
let them not transform into prey

every night from the names grow majestic walls
of homes and streets villages and cities

what is there in our broken villages and cities
Anna Iryna Gorpyna are there no more

translated by Natalya Sukhonos

what is there in our burned-down houses
toys are left there in gardens
whose toys are these
Serhii's Yevhen's Maksym's
Tetiana's Olena's Sara's

what's that under our rickety skies
the last remaining fear is dying
whose was it
Serhii's Artem's Oleh's
Olha's Maryna's Maria's

07.06.2022

translated by John Wright

where do you seek your peace
when you've squeezed out the day like a lemon
where do you drive in the night
as you call out for just a smile at all the checkpoints
where will you seek your death
in what villages and cities
where will you anger your angel
remembering this or that year

peace hides at the bottom
of your palms
of others' pupils
peace lies
where that thin thread pulses on your temple
peace lies so deep
and warms itself in a patch of sun
where irises bloom so white

death sits by your side
doing her cross-stitch and needlepoint
waiting for the next stage
the easiest is anger
the most obvious is acceptance
the stage that isn't on the list
is repentance
if you get to that stage
death loses interest in you
and sympathy

death walks away
and if you look to see
who makes his own hell
on this earth where things are sad enough anyway
you find some papers

that have all your sadness written on them
all your losses and random actions
and each one speaks
as well as it can

and if those papers get taken away
well who are you without them
and what are you seeking
is it peace or is it death
knowing that
in this country
you can't die in peace
without recalling all the dead
without saddening the living

what's on that last paper
nothing
it's only there for whoever
knows how to write down his latest memory
who knows that these papers show nothing but dreams
but freedom's over there
she's planted the whitest irises
and an unknown road
comes up to each tiniest step
just try recognising her now in a crowd

08.06.2022

skin scarred by time is really soft and tender
like the lips touching blossoming peonies
how much longer until you can wear
a baptismal robe again
wake up on somebody's womb and be at peace
listening to her breath
dozing off in the sunlight
savouring old stories that somebody told of us

how much time to let your fingers get lost
in the maze of her wavy hair
to talk and listen
how much more of this
uncharted territory
your time, so precious
how much more of it to not appreciate

no answers
He gives us no answers
He's standing behind our backs so stubborn and tender
whispering
about love
and its unexpected trajectories
and how He is collecting
it all for us
on our way
and we stay silent
all these unbearable days and hours
instead of taking the simplest actions
why oh my Lord when we get it wrong again
does it hurt so much to hear You say
don't go there
stay away
what have I now
acquired
but the shards of my dreams

11.06.2022

I will play on the last strings of the macrame[11] lattice
a full moon of patience and a black cat
all is present
all has come to pass
in the bedroom the aromatic walnut tree's leaves glimmer
somewhere an owl hoots
or maybe it just seems so again

and I will boil dark thick wine
roses that have gone wild press against the old fence
here look it's my shadow
pretending to be happily drunk
and the nagging and quivering scent of climbing flowers

that you witch hide in the bottoms of your pupils
what you saw what you forgot
why did no one ever move from their place
as this requires movement

your past

the strange thing that holds you up with a strong hand
a quiet voice tender features delicate movements
which in that cocktail can in no way grant peace
and you walk and walk
you would not heed anyone like that
like her stories
of deep currents
of wandering from her threshold and all the way
to the garden gate

[11] A form of textile crafting using knotting techniques.

the strange thing pins your heart to the lacework
of virginal grapes
to the latticework of branches bitter dry and full of life
you have no counsel for thoughts of peace or for
the glimmering of a heartbeat
and you seek the gleams of her words as if in a haystack
that don't fit into a line
and in the sunlight of your memory
they are like precious stones
for they seem to belong to you alone

here is a cup of potion brewed for you
well why are you frozen in place
take a sip

13.06.2022

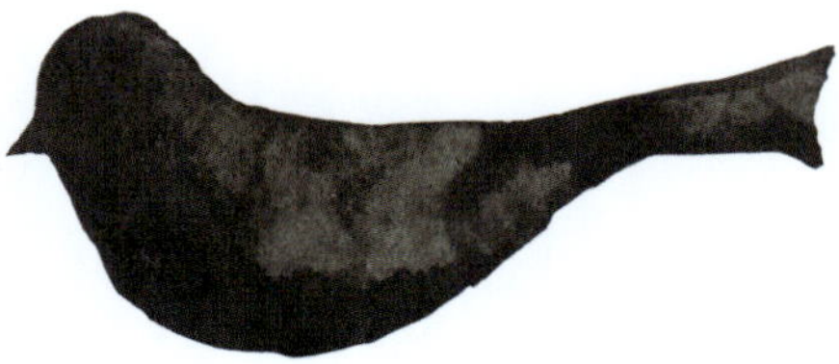

my heart hears a voice in the quiet rumbling of thunder
the voice is toneless strong and filled with sadness
oh my joy keep all your itineraries
don't let anyone know you
but don't let them forget

oh my joy come quietly nearer
let your presence be known
in the quickening clatter of wheels or heartbeat
in the rustle of thin wrapping paper
used to wrap your favourite books and possessions
come to me in a familiar scent
what is that with the delicate scent of sweetness
garden roses
the wind
carried a whiff of their subtle delight

the night
cradles full moon in its palms
oh my joy do what you can
talk to me
in the thundering rumble
the ripe abyss
the familiar voice
turn into a viscous pause

now

and heavens will open their clouds
and it will rain
washing anew the remains
of our hearts and squares
raincoats and shrouds

translated by Anna Antonova

and we will smile again
all of us
the dead the unborn and the living
illusory cards hidden
in our sleeves
capricious transparent watery
guardians of our own joy
and uncertainty

15.06.2022

don't tell them that you were one
with time or water
leaves falling down to the ground
that you woke like winter crops
after those dreadful days
don't tell them
that you had to rise again
after each piercing sound
like a phoenix reborn from the ashes
like steel forged in fire

don't tell them that you were one
with ruinous rains and black storms
the moonlight in our darkest blacked-out nights
streams of love
flowing from one bank card to another
reincarnated as weapons or cars for the frontlines
and that all those regenerations were worth it
worth every second of pain
worth every drop of its ocean

don't tell them
that now you are passing through walls
through the earth and its checkpoints
to share a droplet of water or warmth
to shine like the smallest undimmable star
no matter how hard that may be
love has prevailed over all

time is flying so fast
our blackcurrant is ripening
winter feels like it was days ago
but it's plus thirty-two in the shade
scorching heat until nightfall

translated by Anna Antonova

don't tell them that winter goes on
that all calendar dates don't exist
that cornflowers remind you of the dark sombre sky
blue stars of that crucified february
that your heart is still frozen inside
even though it's june
with rue's bitter scent in the air

don't tell them
that this love has grown so much bigger
than all other loves
and that each part of this city
has your fiercest love deep as ever
both nine-storeyed and two-storeyed buildings
streets and narrow lanes
and pedestrian pathways connecting the suburbs
scoops of flowers that grow in the shade
painted concrete of roadblocks

people
who will fight tooth and nail for each inch
of these gardens and steel
for each thread woven into our flag

16.06.2022

the greatness of what we are living through
how can we fathom
it will take us long years
to comprehend what it means
we'll pour out our pain and our losses
we'll talk through our strength fear and faith
we'll heal our soul wounds with songs
and remember each day
because how could we ever forget

how could we divide it in two
the before and the after
this world that keeps stubbornly spinning
without understanding at all
songs are our painkillers now
don't ask every part of me hurts

we have been all-powerful
for so many long days and hours
how do we know
that our past must be kept
a foe must be repelled
a stray dog must be fed

the most important things happen quietly
while you smoke shielding the light with your hand
and you know how it is
to sleep and wake up at the time of anguish
while the gardens are laden with cherries
ripe as the daily questions you carry
how are you oh Lord
how do you bear these torrents of pain
thank you for asking
I am here

translated by Anna Antonova

with you
He smiles and reloads his gun
look around
you stand for your love and your land
and it's simple
I am on this side
where 'I love you'
comes first

18.06.2022

in the middle of summer right in its very heart
I say a spell for my pain
I note down losses
this centre is like an end and a peculiar beginning
it's love that you will never again look in the eye
for it is everywhere
what should I recall now
what will I recall
as cornflowers and poppies bloomed everywhere
as dirt gathered under fingernails from love
as not a single filthy job is frightening now
as it no longer matters what we will have for lunch
or if lunch will even happen
my love bears a dark sunken mark
and there are even wrinkles under its eyes
here the middle gapes open
it's fragrant
and from every rustle goes a doubled echo
from every word there a doubled strength
did you at least ask for something for yourself
I asked for love
fix that break in me
let me put up all the sails
let me trust in that wave
trust in me as if I'm that thread
that holds the canvas together
trust that I'll hold out
whatever stormy sea or dead calm
the sun pours forth like sparkling wine
to warm us from all sides
those of us who gave ourselves to these streets and avenues
to this earth to this water to these gardens and city squares

translated by Kevin Reese

oh Lord here it is our pilgrimage
don't go anywhere
I am here and I will be here
standing and intertwining my trajectories

21.06.2022

and you run
along a quiet stormy road that sticks to the wheels
race along a stony creek along a green sea of grass
fly away through the exit of birds' wings
go along a thorny path
but don't complain later
don't say to the Lord there is one boundary I couldn't cross
that of my fear and indecision
don't whisper at night what's there now and how is it
don't pester your fellow travellers with questions
how are things there
don't let it interest you so much
listen to the sirens
they're frequent now and thick like baked milk
listen to the siren of the green sea
one of us has already left for you
her arms are long
her heart is cold
her eyes are pitiless
the greatest reward is to him
who was chased by viscid fear into a corner

25.06.2022

translated by Kevin Reese

each day some quiet tasks are added
and your internal composition changes constantly
see before you didn't know how to bear it
but now you haven't slept in days
and you whisper unheard half-asleep
I'll give all that I have

and all that I've had
freedom is given for a bitter price but not the price
of tears at night
not for free and it never falls from the sky
freedom approaches step by step
and weighs even the tiniest desire on its scales
if this is truly your need

these quiet tasks
gather the currants and trim the roses
spend a little time with your friends
be close to whoever you want to hug
where you don't have to talk
quiet tasks committing the maimed streets
and buildings to memory
understanding how much painful love was hiding inside you
stroking this broken stone
take a picture of the unceasingness of life
because it hasn't gone anywhere
it's sitting right next to you and begging to be noticed

quiet tasks
have a cup of coffee downtown
taking notes about changes inside and out
fix the car
to keep driving through this hot and molten city

to its most secret nooks
to bring people some bread
to hide your tears
not to let even a chunk of pain through
quiet tasks
finally to get out from behind the steering wheel
listening to the city
as the missiles fly through it
and listening to how hard that makes it for the city to be silent

25.06.2022

translated by John Wright

along dark roads and barely visible tracks
the train takes me out of the most beautiful of cities
no one can take the city out of me
Kharkiv is like your body
or like you're its body
with Kharkiv it's like your left hand is Bavaria
and your right hand's Nemyshlia[12]
your feet point the way to Osnova
your head is Piatykhatky[13]
in your heart the subway pounds away in the centre of town
your lungs are its airfields and stations
you can't leave it behind or forget it
because it's within you
and everywhere
Saltivka Shyshkivka Velyka Danylivka
Oleksiivka Zaderzhpromya and Holodna Hora[14]
what do you have when you have this city
a shared and happy dream
and as it turns out the matchbox-houses at the Kharkiv Tractor Plant
are the dearest so boundlessly beautiful
and as it turns out each centimetre of the old markets and squares
shows itself to be the most precious thing
and the cobblestones with grass grown up through them
for the first time in a hundred years
your warm and living conscience
in the train a light flashes
its windows are covered tight with curtains
that train is like a glorious night-snake
that train carries me away from the city
under my skin the city is cautiously breathing

26.06.2022

[12]Nemyshlia is a river flowing through Kharkiv.

[13]Bavaria, Osnova and Piatykhatky are neighbourhoods in Kharkiv.

[14]Names of neighbourhoods in Kharkiv.

the sounds are so alike
each one is so much like another
sometimes you wish not to hear or feel them
to know just one thing
to hear just one thing
the sound of the colour of my grass
to say you must live
the sound of the tenderest touch
quietly whispers
you are a priceless creation of woman
the sound of that voice
is forgotten
the place where once there was a trench
is healing
you hear the water coming
it says a terrible thing happened once
and now there's a lake
listen how the earth grows over with grass after that
and again becomes so defenceless
perfectly green
filled with sound
and bitter

28.06.2022

translated by John Wright

translated by Ian Ross Singleton

mama mama tell me about war
not just one story you surely know more
you truly know many
you're quiet again
so I'll go ask tato[15]

tato tato tell me something or other
in school they say big and beautiful sentences
numbers victorious battles dates of events
yet some things the teachers don't know or keep quiet
once our history teacher while talking about
recaptured territories
suddenly ran from the classroom
trying to stop sobbing
what is she crying about tato

tato's quiet too
pats his son with a warm powerful hand
while pressing the steel one into the bone without thinking
son let's talk about that in thirty years
that's a long time tato
son it's just an instant

how do we speak about the war with children not yet born
how do we share what we've seen
what we've heard
they who've been in hell will forever be silent
but we'll talk someday son
because we haven't forgotten

29.06.2022

[15] 'Dad' in Ukrainian.

what awaits us at the border
the exhales of large wagons
resembling grey whales
children
running around in a line between automobiles
cars
that go in a restricted lane with the initials AFU[16]
and the closer we come to the border
the louder the beat of the heart
and the movement of the air
homeward homeward homeward

we desire so much to cross the edge
to converge with the thrum of the tyres
in order finally to stand in the city centre
blasted by every type of missile
to absorb into ourselves the power of the earth and air
to absorb into ourselves the power of ancestry and spirit
to be confirmed in our belief
and make yet another step
a tiny one
towards Victory

02.07.2022

translated by Ian Ross Singleton

[16] The Armed Forces of Ukraine.

translated by Ian Ross Singleton

good day little war, how are things
you know what you've taught me
life's no exercise
not a race
not a test
not a reassessment
life exists here and only today

only today and only at this hour
so that you won't make some kind of stop
even if you're only observing
petting your cat
cooking dinner
mending shoes
give over to this act to the last drop

whether you paint the walkie-talkie
travel by train
learn how to shoot
plant flowers
cast a spell on the enemy
whatever it is there's only a single request
be yourself
value the task as if it's the last one

you know little war what it is that I want
to put on a dress
that's the womanliest
pose for a photo
that's the most delicate
gather together the most beautiful the dearest
and dedicate
my time won in crying and dying
and thus find out that you are now dead

04.07.2022

the woman hasn't seen sun inside since the war started
she shuttered the windows
hung up her dreams
closed all cracks
hammered all nails
it used to be a warm and sunny house
but it became bitter

now it's as if the house is blind
the woman says as she sits on a bench
it's hard to be alone she says
the woman planted the whole garden
planted a patch
made salt-cured salo[17]
says that in february this wasn't enough
now let there be an abundance of all
for children and grandchildren
for those far and near
there'll be enough of her holy gift
the woman blesses the garden
as if the crop depends on this
potatoes or cherries

the woman's bent like an arch
says the sun's setting as am I
all that I know child
the earth will never lead you astray
each one receives their share
children grandchildren kin far and near
you see all abounds
in the Almighty's palm

05.07.2022

translated by Ian Ross Singleton

[17] A Ukrainian culinary speciality consisting of salt-cured pork fatback, sometimes smoked and seasoned with spices. Salo is a staple in Ukrainian households due to its distinct flavour, affordability and long shelf life. It is deeply embedded in the country's culinary and cultural traditions.

brittleness of the strongest people
is sown into their tattoos
here is your charmed day and your crucified night
thousands of stars looking at you
piercing you with their spikes
and you keep thinking
how is my town
are all its stars still looking down
are all its roads still warm
does water still hug the shores at Honcharivska dam[18]
is pavement still as ripe as my home's stone walls
can it still relieve all my woes

people are made of glass and of steel
all at the same time
they can stand firm or they can fall
so like green stars they keep shining at night
those who are still alive
those who cannot sleep
those you've lost and the ones you could keep
lights of your messenger app
like a charm or a lantern

no explanations and no relief
war doesn't let you take a leave
from it
while it lasts
throbbing inside you, a dark lump
thousands of reflections and letters
no matter
in the thick of events
or hundreds of miles away from home
I'm all your days the war whispers

[18]The dam on the Lopan river in Kharkiv that was built in 1934.

driving you mad on weekdays and weekends
every night
I tear your ripe fatigue apart
destroying your city
consistently
I'm all your dusk and your morning glow
quiet or loud
I always want more

quiet only exists
in a pit between your collarbones
when you lie down
your body forgets how to stay asleep
I'm all your days you whisper
there will be no answer
a green messenger light will bloom
like a fern flower
no new messages
yes
you are all my days
even in this bottomless gloom

06.07.2022

whoever seeks the fern flower
covers their tracks
waits out the swelter begs for the cold

a flower
am I
a flower are you

the fence creaked at night
a hoarse voice honed time
don't scream be silent

a flower
am I
a flower are you

day from night night from day
your road elapses
time elapses years pass
others' fears pass into inheritance

a flower
am I
a flower are you

the hedge envelops the fence
constantly surprises the world
whether you're fifteen or forty years old
instead of a thousand words
superior to all treasures

a flower
am I
a flower are you

07.07.2022

translated by Ian Ross Singleton

where have you forsaken me
the heart of my dream
embodiment of God's design
the core of all things
where have you forsaken me

how do you lie beneath the blanket
how do you lie beneath the blanket
the blanket's polyethylene

the shard's five millimetres
the shard's nothing but five millimetres
the shard's so small
it carries death

where will we meet now
where will we meet now
for dead civilians
why an ambulance
where should we rush now
when it has departed from the body

the soul is heavier than the shard
the shard takes out
one soul
at frenzied speed
touches dozens of others

where have you forsaken me
where have you left me
near the place where we
had each other

08.07.2022

translated by Ian Ross Singleton

translated by Ian Ross Singleton

Peter Peter they say you're stone
stiff unwavering steel
Peter how'd you become stone
what rescued you from the fissure
what helped make your stiffness
what saved your obstinacy and your routes

how'd you survive the desert Peter
how'd you undergo the pressure of prison
Peter how can you see everybody attend to their words
and dreams
Peter what's key in this hope and hopelessness
how much did you need to be naïve simple and sincere
to mend the darkness
for it all to come down to faith
to become stiff inside yourself
and be yourself
to liken stone to love

12.07.2022

magpies in flight resemble spindles
in my heart there's just such a spindle
rustling gathering my love into a thread
the spindle of a magpie in the sky spins time's thread
time comes out tender and thin
the war only adds valour to this time

those who are still with me even now
will never ever betray
nor say wait another nine years
or that I have to advise my feelings
they won't cross to the other side of the street or what's real
simply after having thrown away all that's trifling in life
they'll remain

the spindle rustles spins a new world
one that won't be sick or burdensome
we're here everyday
we laugh with each other
give advice about everyday things
fix ourselves
I feel nothing
no confusion
I'll embrace you
in the semblance of all who'll come to embrace
the spindle burns like a match
in order to turn 'I can't take any more'
into

I can take everything in the world
even more

12.07.2022

translated by Ian Ross Singleton

grief is sitting right next to me
scrolling down on her phone
listing the names of her friends and her loved ones
grief has no home
no city
and very few remaining people
grief is looking for names

grief is focused and frail
she can still smile
even though the times have never been darker
grief has an almost-grown child
who's abroad
and a husband from Azovstal[19]
now a prisoner of war
grief keeps whispering the names of survivors
and the ones who didn't get out
and the ones who are dead

grief has learned to appreciate life
its every second and minute
'I will smile for as long as I live
even though it's bitter
and I won't regret it'

grief is gracious and tender
everywhere a stranger
grief is so careful
not to shed as much as a tear

[19] Azovstal is a steel plant in Mariupol, Ukraine, that became notorious during russia's 2022 siege of Mariupol as the last Ukrainian stronghold in the city. After constant russian bombings that lasted for nearly two months and its eventual destruction, Azovstal became a symbol of Ukrainian people's resistance and perseverance.

I hold her tight
and feel the sea waves inside
rippling
the sea of love
and I quietly pray to God
so this fragile woman
could finally feel her grief leaving

15.07.2022

take out all of my splinters
all wreckage and shards
take them out of my heart
where all that is left is the wind
curtains on still-intact window frames
are quietly swaying
the wind imitating
this universe wearing away
please take it out of me
all that is hurting
the bridge of my ribs
is the carving of ages

take it with you
as a charm for good luck
every splinter of pain
like tiny arks
filled with only love

how can I ever
fill the void of my losses
how can I comfort my soul
envelop me in your essence
like healing lake water
like the water of sadness
wash all my sorrows away
toss all my poison aside

I will stand undefeated
a pantheon burned
leave all your doubts behind
Kharkiv
is steel and concrete

18.07.2022

translated by Anna Antonova

love asks of you in human language
mend the gap in my soul with tenderness
pour out my lamentations
pronounce my name
cast out all this anger

love asks of you
heal me
don't undervalue what I've protected
but if you want to kill
aim at me

here's my atonement
by fasting prayer and silence
here's my quiet
that's erased after rocket attacks
here's my goal
never disappearing from radars
here's my strength
to stand in that very place
in one of the scarred cities
and heal it
with myself

18.07.2022

to stop loving people is the least of your tasks
the most infernal of your sins
the world's made by a few simple things
flags echoes and graves
the world waits on change
bands together becomes enraged
by new knowledge and news
the world's full of people yet facing a major decision
and facing God you're all alone

to stop loving people who've plunged into your unconscious
whose names taste bitter on your palate
so you can stand in the wind in the middle of the city
saying names
to contemplate how your armour
thickens and grows in your native city
so you can finally witness how you gave everything
to their names
with abundance or fully

to stop loving people so your memory's wiped
like a worn-out stone in the square
to wait out your part and pardon
to leave each one to their turbulent lives
and contemplate the rain on the street
to try no longer to abide your life
to value the tiniest moment
to stop loving people in spite of how
badly it hurts

21.07.2022

our voices are hoarse from the everyday
                    conversations vows and prayers
new wrinkles appear on the city's skin
new dust circles blemishes
we're coming closer to one another like galaxies
                              by the years days hours
we're standing in every scratched
                              rhythm in every break
between songs
we're standing in every crack between walls
we are those who nurture love
                              having bowed in grief
under ruins
we are those who are becoming invisible
                                  above the springs
under the overstories and the stony slopes
we are those who are concrete and iron
                                in basements deep
those who are so frail and unsteady yet who
                                in war became steel
whose strength is stronger than steel
whose hearts have become torn and enduring

our city like any city any village
is the most important for this country
our voices rasp
we'll win all the same
every city every centimetre of land that's here
even if through the glut of tyranny it disappears
all these hoarse voices
we'll continue to rasp
in every phone conversation

translated by Ian Ross Singleton

in every walkie-talkie
no it's not interference
this is how love talks
this country of yours has matured
                        and sends messages
by Morse code
in new patterns

29.07.2022

the city of heroes Kharkiv
there's bleak news daily
losses nightly
how are you we are asked by others
both far and near
we laugh
we still have a lot to lose
every fighter laid into a grave
an angel pollinates with an antidespairant
the fighter becomes an angel
steps up to guard
embraces at night those close to them
it's not worth it to fall into despair
whispering and breathing in the face
our faces light up thanks to this pollen
thanks to this fighter who took their burden
so important so bitter
thanks to this angel who stands on the shoulders
where all your power comes from
which is immeasurable inexhaustible
and we all carry it
as if we're a bush
no one can burn

31.07.2022

translated by Ian Ross Singleton

I don't want to see it he says but I do every day
I've got a hole inside
and skin tough as bulletproof plates
I am steel and concrete
with bones of heavyweight beams
but I long to wake up one day
and realise it was only a dream

I can't bear to stare at the pain
flooding up their eyes
but it is my own craft my own fight
my Sisyphean task
so I come to the wards bringing marbles
apples and candy
and I ask how they feel and hear back
what is that in your hands
and I shrug as they smile back to me
and I can't help but think
that they must be aware of the essence
of life's simplest things
but they still need to act their part
stay in this childlike mode
so I bring them their toys and their pills
I know the new code

these wards see no crying
but toys can be swapped any day
here hearts turn to mush
and bulletproof plates melt away
as they learn how to walk to believe
and to talk as before
they are not only mine not just patients
just children
not children of war

08.08.2022

that the colour of mourning is actually not black
but rather dark brown
you find that out from how green mixes with blood
that calm's actually not quiet and quiet's not always calm
is revealed since the dead silent march
since the scary loud august
the expectation of victory arrives unheard
when sleep remains beyond the all-encompassing moon
when you order the first books for yourself to the city of heroes
when you are awaiting a message
and there's nowhere in this city
there's no place for you
and the connection is bad

that you're actually not a fighter but rather a helper
a part of civilian armature
a part of the carcass on which muscles thicken
you won't recognise right away

whether chthonic creatures have been vaccinated against rabies
how to survive rabies
to know how much time it needs

how will he die
the one who breaches the chthonic ground
that one will be turned inside-out
and swallowed by history all-a-round

20.08.2022

translated by Ian Ross Singleton

translated by Ian Ross Singleton

how do your actions change the course of the war
how can you protect your dreams from the war
here you wake up and live as if it's not hard
yet another day
let your actions be laughter for those who lose hope
let your hug be a warm sea wave
mighty and strong
your hands make yet another spatial element
an event
the things you do let windows into other lives open
flowers for those who need them

who will help hold the earth for the feet that stand
on the sea bottom
at checkpoints they whisper His call sign
Lord be merciful unto me
I am one of our own

25.08.2022

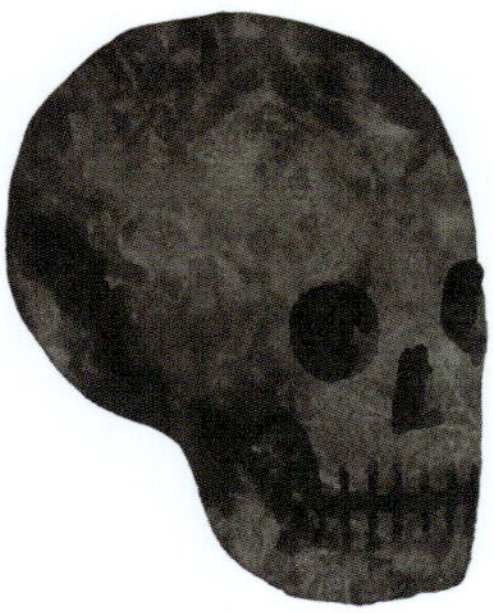

still a long way to swim he says
until that final splash
just keep fixing what's broken
and switching the music you play
just keep packing your army rucksacks
watch bridges blast into air

time is ours now
it's flowing alongside our way
it's calm and it's powerful
pieced together by our faith
our morning prayers
checkpoints marked by children's deaths

still such a long way to swim
till the last splash of water and of applause
we'll write ourselves long-winded letters
about how we are and how it was
to remember later
how we were playing with time
not letting it
pull our most secret veins
from our powerless bodies
how we turned away to brush off our tears
fresh water drops on the windowpane
when we heard words of gratitude
so heartfelt and plentiful
from a time-bent woman with a crooked cane
who was left all alone this horrid black spring

such a long way to swim
my heart
such a long way to swim

26.08.2022

deliver me a bird
tender ornamented with greenish silver
clever and strong
I'll let him out to hunt
deliver me a bird
who's as quiet as the quietest night of august
let his exact iron heart never know any pity
deliver me a bird
he'll defend those I love

tame a fox
every day give it a morsel of meat
what a fox is needed for
will reveal itself with time
trust in its sharp eyes and clever moves
listen to what it will say
and if it's silent
listen to that too
foxes never speak in vain
their voices are deep as their dens
nor do they know pain
nor submission

birds and foxes
are freedom ambassadors
foxes' dens and birds' nests
where's your home Son of man

it burned down

31.08.2022

and they held on to each other as long as they could
old songs flowed in the waters and winds of august
yet they held on
like creeping plants they stuck to shoots of words and melodies
announced 'I know no other way' in every possible manner
weaved their long dialogues with scarcely noted eyelid motions
and the mature weary exhausted sign 'I understand'
a scarcely visible smile 'that's enough'

and as long as they knew the words were mine the notes yours
as long as they smiled at dark nights and piercing mornings
read the news as if swallowing freedom pills
shrugged their shoulders as if they needed another reason
to be joyful at dusk and dawn
apart from the weightiest of reasons
to be present
today
at any one of the porches

translated by Iàn Ross Singleton

01.09.2022

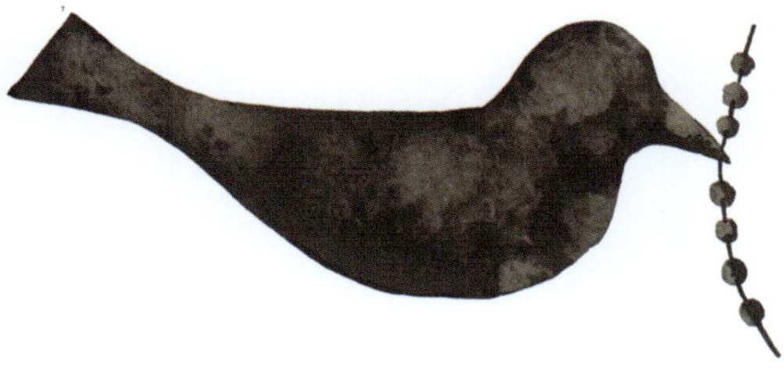

translated by Ian Ross Singleton

the left tributary of the Siversky Donets
the basin of the Sea of Azov
the river Oskil
the Kupiansk and Izium regions
of Kharkiv Oblast
flows southeast of the city of Izium
flows without ceasing

water has a memory
regardless of the current a river whispers names
names of all the unknown buried
a river knows about them from all the underground streams
from the little drops that roll
from the needles in the pine forest
from the rain washing the faces of the living
from the tears mixing with the rain
from the blood soaking this earth more every day

16.09.2022

the same story keeps happening year after year
a baby's first scream is filling the air
the earth the barn and this peopled wilderness
this year the star shines with such clear vividness
since lights are gone and even the earth is blacker
who is breathing so loud in the dark
warm like a blanket
the baby smiles to a stranger
who quietly whispers a psalm
here you are he says accept our earthly alms
we'll bring more tomorrow
unless we're mowed down
by bombs
the baby touches his warm beard
the beard keeps moaning
how did you get stuck out here
just wait little one
a tiny bit more
we'll take you somewhere
where it's warm
and sheaves of wheat are not burning

the same story is now acquiring
new sound and meaning
we waited for Christmas so long
clinging to life
so tell us baby who's born
amid air raid sirens
where is he hiding
this fabled ubiquitous God
did he ever hear or see us
yes he is here

where is here
in Mariupol Izium Bakhmut Hostomel and Kharkiv
what is he doing
working mending and guarding
how can we know him
he's in each one of you everywhere
and He has nothing at all
but your own two hands
the same story is happening year after year
whatever the prophets may tell you
he's born
and he comes to each home
but this time to stay and be there
to the end

25.12.2022

I can see spring enter your city
I can see it rise from the ashes
cast aside its ruins
like an old blanket
after a lengthy sleep
buildings stand naked
walls straighten out
spring
will cloak all hurts
spiky vertebrae bloom
on the spine of this frontier city
dark and deep
enclosed by white mountains
dark waters
green meadows
how are my horses
do they leap
in mighty streams
or rot
in a shallow brook
powerless

24.01.2023

translated by Anna Antonova

translated by Kevin Reese

the heart is disassembled into microns
and reassembled once again
you walk through other people's homes
until the foundation's foundation is revealed
you see it's all simple and we're so simple before God
oh Lord how did you gather yourself up after you died
on the cross
the heaviness of a heavy day drags and drags
why then were there no dressings and haemostatics
why do we have them now but often they make no sense
why do You force the fierce heart to join battle
so many questions so much mute pain
why is Your whisper impossible to hear
what will it tell me instead of You
I am here with you
my heart is flowing with golden veins
it betrays its own knocking
an astonishing craftsman has created a new kintsugi[20]

16.02. 2023

[20]The Japanese art of repairing broken pottery by mending the cracks with lacquer mixed with gold. Kintsugi is often seen as a metaphor for resilience, healing and embracing imperfections.

language of war
brisk impersonal reserved language of love
sign in place of a word
numbers in place of silence
language of war singles out your accomplice
calms your nerves
lulls your heart

in the snowstorm of war we are all accomplices
we call by name each and every city
village and town
river and stream
we say out loud
Izium Volnovakha
Kremenets
Bucha Vovchansk
Kharkiv
we envelop each beloved stone
with its primal names
we purge each grain of sand
whispering
Mariupol Luhansk
Irpin Donetsk Bakhmut
Balakliia Kupiansk
I am here
in each city
village
town
I am
language of love
and language of war
yours
your own

18.02.2023

translated by Anna Antonova

translated by John Wright

witch how did you know this oh how did you know it
that holes in the windows would be covered with blankets
that the earth would grow grey from those shouted curses
that it would be shaken by unstable borders

how did you see it did you dream it or foretell it with cards
that a sincere and pure hearth would warm up the children
that black fire and darkness would destroy people
that the beams of the building forming crosses
would protect them

how was it revealed to you
did you spill the sweetness from the honeysuckle
that the invasion would creep in from all sides
that its bloody thirst is the leader
and Mary's city could not hold out
but would fall

witch how did you see it did you cast bones on a balance
or did the blanket flop funny while you were making the bed
what's the end that you see has the scale been knocked over
the end of the war brings a wind that tastes
like the air after a storm

18.02.2023

the philosophy of your world
and mine has flown apart into pieces
and has sunk down evenly onto the earth
well who are you now
a witch or a moon being
I am a reverberation of a distant universe
the queen of dark curses

I am love and hatred
wheeled out on my tongue
I'm the only one who will never be
'hand in hand'
I am the destruction of the stable laws
of human confinement
I am freedom and will
dreamed-up independence

I go out into the field
to sow blood into the rivers
I am silent and I don't cry
because in my voice there is only emptiness
and there is no music with me
an echo of blind hearts
and a dark shining clot
of fruit-bearing resin

I'm the fabric of the flag
ripped to shreds by the wind
an even row of gravestones
the song is stilled
I am marks made on tombs
beastlike howling in the wood

I'm the fabric of memory
woven by children's hands
migrant girls
in a forgotten village
with a tool found in the attic

I am memory itself

01.03.2023

mother
I've been buried three times this year
I remember the faces of everyone there
twice as a nameless soldier
unknown
but at last I came home

mother don't cry
between that spring and this spring
I kept coming so gently into your dreams
telling you to keep waiting
promising you I'll be found
that I couldn't stay long in that ground

now my promise at last is completed
here's my land
my beloved green fields
you can fly now everyone whispered
I came home on the shield
undefeated

28.03.2023

translated by Anna Antonova

To Anton Derbilov

and the earth will cry for three days
exactly three days
let the rain pour from the sky and herd clouds
in my throat vowels will crowd
and turn grey
dense foggy mist will hang in the air

for three days they'll keep saying your name
talk aloud and cry with no tears
unlike their love tears will run dry
love will sting every word every breath
from plural pronouns
to simply
family

and the congruence of the events and the rain
will reach everywhere
piercing through
oh how we loved you
so defenceless and stubborn
in our memory
apricots will bitterly bloom
forever
white is truly the colour of mourning and death

12.04.2023

DEFYING DESPAIR

Defying despair became my guiding theme during the first year of the full-scale invasion. To document. To reinterpret my experience. To find solid ground underfoot and adjust to a new reality.

For me, poetry is the most immediate art form in the world. It's a tool that allows us to process and reflect on events in the moment of presence – no matter what happens. War, too, yields to poetry.

As the young Ukrainian poet and defender Yevhen Lesin put it: 'When the cannons speak – the Muses pass the ammunition!' This idea resonates deeply with me. I've never understood the old saying, 'When the cannons speak – the Muses fall silent.' How could those who have always stood by us in our darkest hours turn away in wartime and leave us alone with our grief? It simply cannot be.

Ukrainian poets prove every day that poetry persists. It is swift, resilient, unrelenting. It reaches out – to the one who writes, to the one who reads, and even to the one who simply absorbs it.

During the Great War, poetry becomes sustenance – a source of strength and renewal. It's read and written in trenches, under occupation, in cities on the frontlines. Our very way of living now may be a form of poetry – bitter and tender, a story of profound resistance, of our longing and resolve to carry on until the end. 'To endure and to survive.'

To build new bridges, create fresh connections, redraw our inner landscapes – this too is the work of a writer. Sometimes I call it 'constructive poetry', because beyond the written word, there are countless ways to create meaning.

And despair retreats. And strength returns – to move forward and to make anew. Each of our steps leads us closer to Freedom – to live freely on our free land.

Yours,
Natalka Marynchak

AFTERWORD

Natalka Marynchak's *Antidespairant* (*Відчаєспинне*) speaks to us in many voices – a mother watching the bread queues snake past her window, a child asking its parents about war, a dead soldier addressing family members from beyond the grave – all of them mouths of the poem's central figure, 'the city of heroes Kharkiv'. And Kharkiv is not only its people. As Kostiantyn Zorkin brings to life in his remarkable graphics, the city-protagonist is also concrete, steel, fire and non-human animals. It is inseparable from nature – from the cats and foxes that range around its devastated but defiant streets, and the greenery that sprouts from the cracks in its pavements (inhabited by Ukraine's native *mavka* spirits), to the river waters that ensure that this war, its heroism and its atrocities, are not consigned to oblivion:

> water has a memory
> regardless of the current a river whispers names
> names of all the unknown buried

Kharkiv is at once specific and symbolic. The names of the city's streets, squares and districts, recurring almost as a leitmotif, ensure that we know exactly where we are. Intimate, domestic details – a jar of blackcurrant preserve, coffee served in a favourite mug – remind us that the lives of the poem's unnamed human cast are real. Yet the people of Kharkiv represent something far bigger. The dead and the living fight together – 'all our dead stand behind us… we're one whole' – engaged in an epic conflict that to date has raged just over thirty times the duration of the Trojan War. By 16 April 2022, 'the battle lasts three centuries / three centuries and eight years / and a few dozen days'.

The enemy – of which Putin's russia is only the current manifestation – are the faceless, nameless incarnation of the existential threat to the Ukrainian people, their culture and way of life. In the case of the enemy, *Antidespairant* has no tolerance of nuance, no room for the *lacrimae rerum* – they are accursed, and they are to be killed without remorse.

Amid the bloody heroism, the defiance and the violence, we find the sources of hope that give Natalka's poem its name. These manifest themselves in the everyday – the smell of baking bread, the twitching of a cat's tail, birdsong ('the redstart sings and dissolves all sad thoughts') – and are a constant solace. At times, the voice of the poem may seem to falter or entertain doubt, even despair ('we all exist together / and each of us is already tired / of existing'), but the city-protagonist is ultimately self-sustaining, a source of strength and inspiration to itself:

> there is beauty in everything
> even when it seems that beauty
> is gone

* * *

I had the great pleasure of visiting Ukraine on several occasions in 2019, as a guest at the Mystetskyi Arsenal Book Fair in Kyiv, and then working with museums, galleries and individual artists in the capital, Kharkiv, Odessa and Lviv. During my time there I was consistently struck by the dynamism and optimism of so many working in the Arts and Heritage sector, and impressed by the deep pool of talent in the country, especially among the young.

Kulturalis is proud to publish this beautiful, important book, and to be associated with Natalka whose words are worth repeating in the context of our commitment to supporting and promoting the cultures of the world:

> Culture defines a nation – it gives it solid ground beneath its feet. And as it turns out, in war's most difficult days, the nation turns to its culture with open arms, thirsting for all of its gifts, past and present.

We hope that this book will play its part in ensuring that the violation of Ukraine is not forgotten, and does not go unpunished. *Відчаєспинне* is a remedy not only against despair, but against complacency, ignorance and misinformation.

* * *

On behalf of Kulturalis, I dedicate this publication to all our friends from Ukraine and elsewhere who have made this project possible: Oleksandr Savchuk and Daiana Sheludkevych; Natalka Marynchak and Kostiantyn Zorkin; Anna Antonova, Kevin Reese, Ian Ross Singleton, Natalya Sukhonos and John Wright; my business partner Charlotte Kramer, who generously sponsored the book; and Iryna Baturevych of Chytomo.com, who was my first guide when I arrived in Kyiv in 2019 and last year introduced me to Oleksandr Savchuk at the Frankfurt Book Fair. I would also like to thank the following people I have had the pleasure of working with during my visits to Ukraine and since: Kateryna Chuyeva, Liudmyla Gubianuri, Semen Kantor, Zhanna and Yevhen Karas, Oksana Khmelyovska, Kateryna Levchenko, Liudmyla Liakhevych, Grace Mahoney, Olenka Martynyuk, Sviatoslav Mykhailov, Oleksandr Mykhed, Sofronis Paradeisopoulos, Oksana Schur, Valeria Shevchenko, Liudmyla Strokova, Valeriy Suntsov, Niki Théron, Iryna Vorobiova and Taras Voznyak. Many we are currently working with; at least one is now living in London; our best wishes and prayers go to those with whom we have lost contact, and those we know are continuing to resist the enemy in their homeland.

Neil Titman
Managing Director, Kulturalis
Tangier, 3 July 2025

ABOUT THE AUTHORS

Natalka Marynchak

Poet, writer, translator, volunteer and radio host. Born in Kharkiv, Ukraine.

Author of several poetry collections, including *NestrymN2O, Stop.ua, Antidespairant* and *Temporary Crossing*.

She is also the author of the non-fiction book *Lullaby for the 21st Century: What Soothes You to Sleep?*, the multimedia project *Third Children* (a record and a book), and co-author of the graphic novel *In the Name of the City*.

Marynchak has translated and rhythmically adapted chamber operas from English into Ukrainian, including *The Medium* by Gian Carlo Menotti and *The Man Who Mistook His Wife for a Hat* by minimalist composer Michael Nyman. She also translated Dmytro Ternovyi's play *Hamlet.Show*, among others.

Kostiantyn Zorkin

A multidisciplinary artist working across performance, installation, puppet theatre, graphic arts, sculpture and land art.

A graduate in Culturology from the Kharkiv Academy of Culture, he is also a scenographer and educator.

Zorkin's practice is grounded in the use of natural materials – wood, metal, ink and paper – employing manual techniques to shape and transform them. His works reinterpret the magical and mythological functions of art, constructing a personal symbolic system of signs and gestures.

Key projects include *Protective Layer* (2022–3), the puppet performance *Giraffe Mons* (2023), the graphic novel *In the Name of the City* (2024) and illustrations for Adela Knapova's book *Bloody Compote* (2025). He lives and works in Kharkiv.

CONTENTS

Originally published in 2023 in Kharkiv, Ukraine,
by Oleksandr Savchuk Publishing House,
under the title *Відчаєспинне* (*Vidchaiespynne*)
www.savchook.com · savchook.book@gmail.com

EU GPSR Authorised Representative:
EASY ACCESS SYSTEM EUROPE OÜ,
Mustamäe tee 50, 10621, TALLINN, Estonia
email: info@easproject.org

Kulturalis Ltd, 14 Old Queen Street,
London SW1H 9HP, United Kingdom
www.kulturalis.com · info@kulturalis.com
ISBN 978-1-83636-036-0

Translated by Anna Antonova, Kevin Reese,
Ian Ross Singleton, Natalya Sukhonos and John Wright.

Designed and set by Oleksandr Savchuk in Mariupol typeface.

Reprographics by Oleksandr Savchuk.

Printed and bound in Turkey.

10 9 8 7 6 5 4 3 2 1